HOW TO WIN AT FOREX TRADING EASILY, EVERY TIME

Top Secrets, Tips And Best Strategies For Winning Big

Copyright © 2023, Frank Albert

No part of this book may be reproduced or transmitted in any form or by any means, electronic or mechanical, including photocopying, recording, or by any information storage and retrieval system, without written permission from the copyright owner.

All Rights Reserved

Disclaimer

The information presented in this book is intended for educational and informational purposes only. The strategies, tips, and secrets shared in this book are based on the author's experience and research, but there is no guarantee of specific results or profits. Forex trading involves inherent risks, and readers are advised to conduct their own analysis, seek professional advice, and carefully consider their financial situation before engaging in any trading activities. The author and publisher disclaim any liability for any losses or damages incurred as a result of the information provided in this book. It is important to approach forex trading with caution and only invest what you can afford to lose.

CHAPTERS

CHAPTER 1: THE FOREX MARKET: AN OVERVIEW

CHAPTER 2: DEVELOPING A WINNING MINDSET

CHAPTER 3: SETTING REALISTIC GOALS AND CREATING A TRADING PLAN

CHAPTER 4: UNDERSTANDING RISK MANAGEMENT AND MONEY MANAGEMENT

CHAPTER 5: MASTERING TECHNICAL ANALYSIS

CHAPTER 6: USING FUNDAMENTAL ANALYSIS TO YOUR ADVANTAGE

CHAPTER 7: CHOOSING THE RIGHT TRADING STRATEGY FOR YOU

CHAPTER 8: UTILIZING EFFECTIVE ENTRY AND EXIT STRATEGIES

CHAPTER 9: MANAGING EMOTIONS AND AVOIDING IMPULSIVE TRADING

CHAPTER 10: CONTINUAL LEARNING AND IMPROVEMENT IN FOREX TRADING

"Winning at forex trading is not about luck; it's about skill, analysis, and careful decision-making."

Kathy Lien

CHAPTER 1

THE FOREX MARKET: AN OVERVIEW

The forex market, also known as the foreign exchange market, is the largest and most liquid financial market in the world. It operates 24 hours a day, five days a week, allowing traders to engage in currency exchange on a global scale.

This chapter details a comprehensive overview of the forex market, its participants, and its unique characteristics.

The forex market serves as a platform for individuals, corporations, financial institutions, and governments to exchange one currency for another. Its primary function is to facilitate international trade and investment by enabling the conversion of currencies at determined exchange rates.

Unlike other financial markets, such as the stock market, the forex market does not have a centralized exchange. Instead, it operates as an over-the-counter (OTC) market, where transactions are conducted electronically between participants through a global network of banks, brokers, and financial institutions.

One of the key features of the forex market is its high liquidity.

With a daily trading volume of over $6 trillion, there is a constant flow of buyers and sellers, ensuring that traders can enter and exit positions at any time with minimal price slippage.

This liquidity also means that traders have the opportunity to profit from both rising and falling markets.

The forex market is composed of various participants, each with different objectives and motivations. The main players in the forex market include commercial banks, central banks, hedge funds, multinational corporations, and retail traders. Commercial banks, as the primary liquidity providers, account for a significant portion of the market volume. Central banks play a crucial role in influencing exchange rates through monetary policies and interventions. Hedge funds and multinational corporations engage in forex trading to manage their international transactions and investments. Lastly, retail traders, like individual investors, participate in the market through online brokers and trading platforms.

Currencies are traded in pairs, with the most actively traded pairs referred to as major currency pairs. These pairs typically involve the U.S. dollar (USD) against another major currency, such as the euro (EUR), Japanese yen (JPY), British pound (GBP), or Swiss franc (CHF).

In addition to major currency pairs, there are also minor currency pairs and exotic currency pairs, which involve less traded or emerging market currencies.

The forex market operates continuously from Monday to Friday, starting with the opening of the Asian session in Tokyo, followed by the European session in London, and finally the North American session in New York. As different sessions overlap, there are periods of increased volatility and trading activity. Traders often strategize to take advantage of these trading sessions and optimize their trading opportunities.

Summarily, understanding the forex market is essential for any trader looking to succeed in forex trading. It is a dynamic and decentralized market with immense liquidity, allowing traders to capitalize on global currency fluctuations. By grasping the fundamentals of the forex market and its participants, you will be better prepared to navigate its intricacies and develop effective trading strategies.

"The true measure of success in forex trading is not the size of your wins, but how you handle your losses."

Jesse Livermore

CHAPTER 2

DEVELOPING A WINNING MINDSET

Developing a winning mindset is a crucial aspect of achieving success in forex trading. While technical analysis, fundamental analysis, and trading strategies play essential roles, it is the trader's mindset that ultimately determines their ability to consistently make profitable decisions.

This chapter explores the key elements of a winning mindset and provides practical tips for developing mental resilience and discipline in the forex market.

Embrace a Growth Mindset

A growth mindset is the belief that abilities and skills can be developed through dedication and effort. Embracing this mindset allows traders to view failures and setbacks as learning opportunities rather than personal deficiencies. By focusing on continuous learning and improvement, traders can adapt to changing market conditions and refine their trading strategies.

Set Realistic Expectations

Setting realistic expectations is crucial for maintaining emotional balance in forex trading.

It is essential to understand that forex trading is not a get-rich-quick scheme but a long-term endeavor that requires patience and persistence.

By setting realistic goals and accepting that losses are an inevitable part of trading, traders can avoid impulsive decisions driven by greed or fear.

Develop Self-Discipline

Self-discipline is the foundation of a winning mindset. It involves following a trading plan consistently, sticking to predefined risk management rules, and avoiding impulsive trades.

Developing self-discipline requires establishing a routine, managing time effectively, and staying committed to the trading process, even during periods of market volatility or challenging trading conditions.

Manage Emotions

Emotions can significantly impact trading decisions. Fear and greed are common emotions that can cloud judgment and lead to irrational trading choices. Successful traders learn to manage their emotions by developing self-awareness and implementing strategies to maintain emotional equilibrium.

Techniques such as meditation, deep breathing exercises, and journaling can help traders remain calm and focused during trading sessions.

Practice Patience

Patience is a virtue in forex trading. Waiting for the right trading setups and avoiding impulsive trades based on emotions or short-term market fluctuations is essential for long-term success.

Patience allows traders to take a systematic and disciplined approach, leading to better risk management and higher-quality trades.

Cultivate a Positive Attitude

Maintaining a positive attitude is crucial for staying motivated and resilient in the face of challenges. Positive self-talk, visualization techniques, and surrounding oneself with supportive and like-minded individuals can help cultivate a positive mindset. Believing in one's abilities and maintaining optimism even during periods of losses can contribute to overall trading success.

Accept Responsibility

Successful traders take full responsibility for their trading decisions and outcomes. They understand that they are in control of their actions and that blaming external factors or circumstances does not lead to growth.

Taking responsibility enables traders to learn from mistakes, make necessary adjustments, and continuously improve their trading performance.

Practice Consistency

Consistency is key in forex trading. Following a consistent routine, trading plan, and risk management strategies builds discipline and enhances decision-making skills.

Consistency also allows traders to track their progress, identify patterns, and make informed adjustments to their trading strategies over time.

Learn from Losses

Losses are an inevitable part of trading, and successful traders approach them as learning opportunities rather than failures. Analyzing losing trades objectively, identifying mistakes or weaknesses, and making adjustments to avoid similar situations in the future is crucial for continuous improvement. Learning from losses helps traders refine their strategies and develop resilience in the face of adversity.

Practice Self-Care

Taking care of oneself physically and mentally is vital for maintaining a winning mindset. Traders need to prioritize proper nutrition, regular exercise, and sufficient rest to optimize cognitive function and emotional well-being.

Engaging in activities outside of trading, such as hobbies, spending time with loved ones, and pursuing personal interests, helps maintain a healthy work-life balance and prevents burnout.

In a nutshell, developing a winning mindset is fundamental to achieving success in forex trading. By embracing a growth mindset, setting realistic expectations, cultivating self-discipline, managing emotions, and practicing patience and consistency, traders can enhance their decision-making abilities and improve their overall trading performance. Building a winning mindset takes time and effort, but the rewards in terms of long-term profitability and personal growth are well worth it.

"Success in forex trading is not about the number of wins you achieve, but the consistency of your profitability."

Anonymous

CHAPTER 3

SETTING REALISTIC GOALS AND CREATING A TRADING PLAN

Setting realistic goals and creating a well-defined trading plan are essential steps for success in forex trading. Without clear objectives and a structured approach, traders may find themselves aimlessly navigating the market, making impulsive decisions that can lead to inconsistent results.

In this chapter, we explore the importance of goal setting and provide guidance on how to create an effective trading plan that aligns with your objectives.

Setting Realistic Goals

> Before diving into the forex market, it is crucial to establish realistic goals that align with your trading aspirations.
>
> Setting goals provides a sense of direction and purpose, allowing you to measure progress and stay motivated. However, it is essential to set goals that are achievable and based on sound reasoning rather than unrealistic expectations.

- Define Your Purpose

Start by identifying your purpose for trading. Is it to generate additional income, achieve financial independence, or simply gain a deeper understanding of the financial markets?

Defining your purpose will help you establish clear goals that are meaningful to you and keep you focused on the bigger picture.

- Set Specific and Measurable Goals

  Goals should be specific and measurable to provide clarity and allow for progress tracking.

  For example, instead of setting a vague goal like "make money from forex trading," set specific targets such as "achieve a monthly profit of 5% on average" or "reach a specific account balance within a certain time frame."

- Break It Down

  Break down your larger goals into smaller, actionable steps. This approach allows you to focus on manageable tasks and gives you a sense of accomplishment as you achieve each milestone.

  For instance, if your goal is to achieve a certain annual return, break it down into monthly or weekly targets to help you stay on track.

Creating a Trading Plan

A trading plan is a comprehensive document that outlines your approach to trading, including your strategies, risk management rules, and guidelines for entering and exiting trades.

It serves as a roadmap, providing structure and discipline to your trading activities. Here are the key elements to consider when creating your trading plan:

- Trading Strategies

    Clearly define the trading strategies you will employ. This could include technical analysis, fundamental analysis, or a combination of both. Identify the indicators, chart patterns, or economic events you will use to make trading decisions.

- Risk Management

    Establishing effective risk management rules is crucial to protect your trading capital and minimize losses. Determine your maximum acceptable risk per trade, set stop-loss orders to limit potential losses, and define your position sizing strategy.

    Consider incorporating risk-reward ratios to ensure that potential profits outweigh potential losses.

- Trading Timeframes

    Decide on the timeframes you will trade based on your available time and trading preferences.

Will you focus on short-term intraday trades, medium-term swing trades, or longer-term position trades?

Selecting a timeframe that aligns with your schedule and trading style is essential for consistency.

- Entry and Exit Criteria

    Clearly define the criteria for entering and exiting trades. This could involve specific price levels, technical indicators, or fundamental factors.

    Set rules for entering trades based on specific market conditions and establish profit targets or trailing stop-loss levels to secure gains and limit losses.

- Record Keeping and Analysis

    Establish a system for recording and analyzing your trades. Maintain a trading journal to document your trades, including the reasons for entering and exiting positions, your emotions during the trade, and any lessons learned.

    Regularly review your trading journal to identify patterns, strengths, and weaknesses in your trading approach.

- Market Analysis Routine

    Define a routine for conducting market analysis.

Determine the frequency and timeframes for reviewing charts, economic calendars, and news updates. Incorporate a systematic approach to stay informed about market trends, economic events, and potential trading opportunities.

- Review and Adjust

    Regularly review and assess the effectiveness of your trading plan. As you gain experience and market conditions change, you may need to make adjustments to your strategies, risk management rules, or trading timeframe. Be open to refining your plan to adapt to evolving market dynamics.

Remember, a trading plan is a dynamic document that should evolve with your trading journey. Continuously monitor and update it to reflect your growing knowledge and experience in the forex market.

As a recap, setting realistic goals and creating a comprehensive trading plan are essential steps towards success in forex trading. Clear objectives provide focus and motivation, while a well-defined trading plan brings structure and discipline to your trading activities. By setting achievable goals and outlining your strategies, risk management rules, and entry/exit criteria, you will be better equipped to navigate the forex market with a systematic and disciplined approach. Regularly review and adjust your plan as needed to adapt to changing market conditions and your evolving trading skills.

"The biggest victory in forex trading is mastering your emotions and staying calm amidst market turbulence."

Mark Douglas

CHAPTER 4

UNDERSTANDING RISK MANAGEMENT AND MONEY MANAGEMENT

Effective risk management and money management are vital components of successful forex trading. While identifying profitable trading opportunities is important, it is equally crucial to protect your trading capital and preserve long-term sustainability.

In this chapter, we explore the principles of risk management and money management, providing valuable insights on how to safeguard your funds and optimize your trading performance.

Risk Management

Risk management involves assessing and mitigating potential risks associated with trading activities. By implementing proper risk management techniques, traders can protect their capital from significant losses and ensure the longevity of their trading endeavors.

Below are key principles to consider for effective risk management:

➢ **Define Risk Tolerance:** Assess your risk tolerance level before entering trades. It is crucial to understand how much loss you can comfortably withstand without compromising your emotional well-being or overall trading strategy. Avoid risking more than you can afford to lose, as it can lead to irrational decision-making and emotional turmoil.

➢ **Set Stop-Loss Orders:** Implementing stop-loss orders is an essential risk management practice. A stop-loss order is a predetermined price level at which you will exit a trade to limit potential losses. By placing stop-loss orders, you ensure that any losses are contained within your predetermined risk tolerance.

➢ **Determine Position Sizing:** Position sizing refers to the allocation of a specific portion of your trading capital to each trade. It is essential to determine an appropriate position size based on your risk tolerance and the potential risk of the trade. By avoiding excessive position sizes, you limit the impact of any individual trade on your overall portfolio.

➢ **Use Risk-Reward Ratios:** Assess the potential risk versus reward of each trade using risk-reward ratios. A risk-reward ratio compares the potential profit of a trade to the potential loss. It helps you identify trades with a favorable risk-reward profile, where the potential reward is significantly higher than the potential risk.

> **Diversify Your Portfolio:** Spreading your capital across different currency pairs and non-correlated assets can help mitigate risk. Diversification can reduce the impact of adverse price movements in any particular market, as losses in one area may be offset by gains in another.

Money Management

Money management involves the overall management and allocation of your trading capital. It focuses on optimizing your trading performance by effectively utilizing your funds. Consider the following principles for effective money management:

- ❖ Establish a Capital Preservation Mindset

    Prioritize the preservation of your trading capital above all else. Protecting your capital from significant losses is crucial for long-term success. Be disciplined and avoid taking unnecessary risks that could jeopardize your account balance.

- ❖ Determine Risk-to-Reward Ratios

    Assess the potential risk-to-reward ratios of your trades. Aim for trades where the potential reward is significantly higher than the potential risk. This ensures that, over a series of trades, your winning trades are more profitable than your losing trades, allowing you to maintain a positive overall account balance.

- ❖ Use Leverage Wisely

    If utilizing leverage, do so responsibly and with caution. While leverage can amplify profits, it also magnifies losses. Ensure that you fully understand the implications of leverage and use it within your risk tolerance. Be conservative in your leverage usage to prevent excessive exposure.

- ❖ Monitor Account Equity

    Regularly monitor your account equity to assess your overall financial performance. This allows you to identify any potential issues, such as excessive losses or declining profitability, and take appropriate actions to address them.

- ❖ Avoid Overtrading

    Overtrading can lead to excessive transaction costs and emotional exhaustion. Stick to your trading plan and avoid entering trades that do not meet your predetermined criteria.

    Quality over quantity is crucial in maintaining consistent trading performance.

- ❖ Regularly Withdraw Profits

    As your trading account grows, consider withdrawing a portion of your profits regularly. This allows you to enjoy the fruits of your labor and further safeguard your capital.

Additionally, withdrawing profits can provide psychological benefits, as it reinforces the notion that trading is a profitable endeavor.

❖ Continuously Educate Yourself

Invest in your trading education and stay updated on market developments. Expanding your knowledge and skills enhances your ability to make informed decisions and adapt to changing market conditions.

Summarily, effective risk management and money management are essential for sustainable success in forex trading. By implementing risk management techniques such as defining risk tolerance, setting stop-loss orders, determining position sizing, and using risk-reward ratios, you can protect your capital and limit losses. Additionally, practicing sound money management principles, such as capital preservation, risk-to-reward analysis, responsible use of leverage, and regular profit withdrawals, optimizes your trading performance and enhances long-term profitability. Remember, managing risk and capital is a continuous process that requires discipline, adaptability, and a commitment to ongoing learning.

"To win in forex trading, you must be willing to accept losses as part of the learning process and move forward with determination."

Alexander Elder

CHAPTER 5

MASTERING TECHNICAL ANALYSIS

Technical analysis is a powerful tool in forex trading that helps traders make informed decisions based on historical price data and market patterns. By mastering the art of technical analysis, traders can gain valuable insights into market trends, identify potential entry and exit points, and enhance their overall trading accuracy.

In this chapter, we delve into the world of technical analysis, exploring its key principles and providing strategies to help you become proficient in analyzing price charts.

Understanding Price Charts

Price charts are the foundation of technical analysis. They display historical price data in various formats, such as line charts, bar charts, and candlestick charts.

Each chart type has its advantages, but candlestick charts are widely used due to their ability to provide a comprehensive view of price action, including open, high, low, and close prices for a given period.

Key Chart Patterns

Chart patterns are visual representations of price movements that repeat over time. Mastering chart patterns can help you anticipate market reversals and identify potential trading opportunities.

Some common chart patterns include:

- ❖ Support and Resistance

Support levels indicate price levels where buying pressure is expected to emerge, preventing further price declines. Resistance levels, on the other hand, represent price levels where selling pressure is expected to arise, preventing further price increases. Understanding support and resistance levels helps traders identify potential entry and exit points.

- ❖ Trendlines

Trendlines connect consecutive highs or lows in a price chart. Upward-sloping trendlines indicate an uptrend, while downward-sloping trendlines indicate a downtrend. Drawing trendlines correctly allows traders to visualize the direction of the market and potentially identify trend reversals.

- ❖ Chart Patterns

Chart patterns, such as head and shoulders, double tops, double bottoms, and triangles, provide valuable insights into potential trend reversals or continuation. By recognizing these patterns, traders can make informed decisions on when to enter or exit trades.

Indicators and Oscillators

Technical indicators and oscillators are mathematical calculations applied to price charts.

They provide additional information to help traders confirm trends, identify overbought or oversold conditions, and generate trading signals.

Some commonly used indicators include:

- Moving Averages

Moving averages smooth out price data and help identify trend direction. Traders use different time periods for moving averages, such as 50-day, 100-day, or 200-day moving averages, to gauge short-term or long-term trends.

- Relative Strength Index (RSI)

RSI is an oscillator that measures the speed and change of price movements. It helps traders identify overbought or oversold conditions, which can signal potential reversals.

- Bollinger Bands

Bollinger Bands consist of a moving average line and upper and lower bands that represent standard deviations from the moving average. They help identify periods of high or low volatility and potential price breakouts.

- MACD (Moving Average Convergence Divergence)

MACD is a trend-following momentum indicator that shows the relationship between two moving averages. It helps traders identify potential trend reversals and generate buy or sell signals.

Multiple Time Frame Analysis

Using multiple time frames for analysis is a powerful technique in technical analysis. By analyzing price action across different time frames, traders gain a comprehensive understanding of the overall trend and can fine-tune their entry and exit points.

For example, using a higher time frame for trend identification and a lower time frame for precise entry timing can enhance trading accuracy.

Backtesting and Forward Testing

Backtesting involves analyzing historical data to assess the effectiveness of a trading strategy. By applying your trading rules to past data, you can evaluate the profitability and consistency of your strategy.

Forward testing involves implementing your strategy in real-time trading with a small position size to validate its performance.

Both techniques help traders gain confidence in their strategies and make necessary adjustments to improve results.

Continual Learning and Adaptation

The field of technical analysis is vast and ever-evolving. To master it, traders must commit to continual learning and adaptation. Stay updated with new chart patterns, indicators, and strategies.

Attend webinars, read books, and follow respected traders who share their insights. Incorporate new techniques into your analysis and adapt your approach as market conditions change.

Remember, technical analysis is not foolproof and should be used in conjunction with other forms of analysis, such as fundamental analysis and market sentiment. Develop a well-rounded trading approach that combines various tools and techniques to make more informed trading decisions.

In a nutshell, mastering technical analysis is essential for successful forex trading. By understanding price charts, recognizing key chart patterns, utilizing indicators and oscillators, performing multiple time frame analysis, and incorporating backtesting and forward testing, traders can gain a deeper understanding of market trends and enhance their trading accuracy. Continual learning and adaptation are crucial to staying ahead in the dynamic world of technical analysis. By honing your technical analysis skills, you increase your chances of making informed and profitable trading decisions in the forex market.

"The most important quality for a forex trader to possess is the ability to stay focused and disciplined."

Jack D. Schwager

CHAPTER 6

USING FUNDAMENTAL ANALYSIS TO YOUR ADVANTAGE

Fundamental analysis is a powerful approach to forex trading that involves evaluating economic, social, and political factors to determine the intrinsic value of a currency. By understanding the underlying forces that drive currency movements, traders can make informed decisions and capitalize on long-term trends.

In this chapter, we explore the key principles of fundamental analysis and provide strategies to help you use it to your advantage.

Economic Indicators

Economic indicators provide valuable insights into the health and performance of an economy. They help traders assess the overall strength of a currency and its potential for appreciation or depreciation.

Some key economic indicators to consider include:

- ❖ Gross Domestic Product (GDP)

GDP measures the total value of goods and services produced within a country's borders.

A growing GDP generally indicates a strong economy and may lead to currency appreciation.

- ❖ Interest Rates

Central banks adjust interest rates to control inflation and stimulate or slow down economic growth. Higher interest rates can attract foreign investors and strengthen a currency, while lower rates may have the opposite effect.

- ❖ Employment Data

Employment figures, such as non-farm payrolls and unemployment rates, provide insights into the labor market's health. Strong employment data often leads to economic growth and can support currency strength.

- ❖ Inflation

Inflation measures the rate at which prices for goods and services rise. High inflation erodes the purchasing power of a currency and can lead to currency depreciation.

- ❖ Central Bank Policy

Central banks play a crucial role in shaping a country's monetary policy. Monitoring central bank announcements, such as interest rate decisions and monetary policy statements, can provide valuable insights into future currency movements.

Market Sentiment

Market sentiment refers to the overall attitude and perception of market participants towards a particular currency. It can greatly influence currency prices, sometimes even more than fundamental factors.

Traders can gauge market sentiment through various methods, including:

- News and Economic Releases

Stay updated with news releases, economic data, and geopolitical events that can impact market sentiment. Positive news can boost confidence and lead to currency appreciation, while negative news can have the opposite effect.

- Sentiment Indicators

Sentiment indicators, such as the Commitment of Traders (COT) report, measure the positions of major market participants, such as commercial traders, institutional investors, and speculators. Analyzing these indicators can provide insights into market sentiment and potential currency movements.

Geopolitical Factors

Geopolitical events, such as elections, geopolitical tensions, trade agreements, and policy changes, can significantly impact currency values.

Traders should stay informed about global political developments and their potential implications on the forex market.

For example:

- Elections: Political stability and the outcome of elections can affect market sentiment and currency values. Changes in government leadership or policies may lead to uncertainty and currency volatility.

- Trade Agreements: Trade agreements, such as free trade agreements or tariffs imposed on imports, can impact currency values. Positive trade developments can boost currency strength, while trade disputes may lead to currency depreciation.

- Policy Changes: Changes in fiscal or monetary policies can have a substantial impact on a country's economy and currency. Pay attention to policy announcements and their potential implications on currency values.

Intermarket Analysis

Intermarket analysis involves examining the relationships between different financial markets, such as stocks, bonds, commodities, and currencies. By analyzing these intermarket relationships, traders can gain insights into potential currency movements.

For example:

- Equity Markets: Strong performance in equity markets may indicate positive investor sentiment and lead to currency appreciation, while declining stock markets may signal risk aversion and currency depreciation.

- Bond Yields: Higher bond yields can attract foreign investors seeking higher returns and strengthen a currency, while lower yields may have the opposite effect.

- Commodity Prices: Commodity prices, especially those of commodities tied to a particular currency's export or import, can impact currency values. For example, a rise in oil prices may support currencies of oil-exporting countries.

Long-Term Trends

Fundamental analysis is particularly useful for identifying long-term trends in the forex market. By understanding the fundamental factors that drive currency values, traders can position themselves to profit from prolonged trends.

Monitor economic data, geopolitical developments, and central bank policies to identify long-term opportunities.

Combining Fundamental and Technical Analysis

While fundamental analysis focuses on long-term trends, technical analysis is valuable for short-term trading decisions.

Combining the two approaches can provide a comprehensive view of the market. Use fundamental analysis to identify long-term trends and technical analysis to fine-tune entry and exit points.

Summarily, fundamental analysis is a powerful tool for forex traders. By understanding economic indicators, monitoring market sentiment, staying informed about geopolitical factors, conducting intermarket analysis, and identifying long-term trends, traders can make informed decisions and position themselves for success in the forex market. Remember to integrate fundamental analysis with other forms of analysis and continually update your knowledge to adapt to ever-changing market dynamics.

"Consistency and patience are key to achieving long-term success in forex trading."

Andrei Knight

CHAPTER 7

CHOOSING THE RIGHT TRADING STRATEGY FOR YOU

In the world of forex trading, there is no one-size-fits-all strategy. Each trader is unique, with different goals, risk tolerance, and trading preferences. Choosing the right trading strategy is crucial to your success as a forex trader. It involves understanding your strengths, evaluating different strategies, and selecting the approach that aligns with your personality and trading style.

In this chapter, we explore the process of choosing the right trading strategy for you.

Know Yourself

Before diving into different trading strategies, take the time to understand yourself as a trader.

You can ask yourself the following questions:

- ✓ What are your financial goals? Are you looking for short-term gains or long-term wealth accumulation?

- ✓ What is your risk tolerance? How much capital are you willing to risk on each trade?

- ✓ What is your trading experience? Are you a beginner or an experienced trader?

- ✓ What is your preferred time commitment? Are you looking to trade on a part-time basis or dedicate more time to active trading?

- ✓ What is your psychological makeup? Are you patient and disciplined, or do you prefer quick action and excitement?

Understanding your goals, risk tolerance, experience, time commitment, and psychological traits will help you narrow down your options and choose a strategy that suits you best.

Explore Different Trading Strategies

Once you have a clear understanding of yourself as a trader, it's time to explore different trading strategies.

Below are some popular strategies to consider:

- ➢ **Scalping:** Scalping involves making numerous short-term trades to capture small price movements. Scalpers aim to accumulate small profits quickly and rely on high trading frequency.

- ➢ **Day Trading:** Day trading involves opening and closing trades within a single trading day. Day traders take advantage of intraday price fluctuations and often close all positions before the market closes.

- **Swing Trading:** Swing trading involves holding trades for several days to weeks. Swing traders aim to capture larger price movements and are willing to tolerate short-term market fluctuations.

- **Position Trading:** Position trading involves holding trades for weeks to months, or even longer. Position traders focus on long-term trends and often base their decisions on fundamental analysis.

- **Breakout Trading:** Breakout trading involves entering trades when price breaks through significant support or resistance levels. Breakout traders aim to catch strong price movements after consolidation phases.

- **Trend Following:** Trend following strategies involve identifying and riding established trends. Traders using this strategy aim to profit from the continuation of existing trends.

- **Range Trading:** Range trading involves identifying price ranges in which a currency pair is trading and buying at support levels and selling at resistance levels.

- **Carry Trading:** Carry trading involves taking advantage of interest rate differentials between two currencies. Traders earn interest by holding positions in higher-yielding currencies while simultaneously selling lower-yielding currencies.

- **Automated Trading:** Automated trading involves using computer programs or algorithms to execute trades based on predetermined criteria. It can incorporate various strategies and is suitable for traders who prefer a systematic approach.

Research and study each strategy to understand its principles, advantages, and limitations. Consider demo trading or backtesting each strategy to see how it aligns with your trading style and goals.

Match Strategy with Personality and Lifestyle

After exploring different strategies, match them with your personality and lifestyle.

Below are some considerations to keep in mind:

- Time Commitment

    If you have limited time to dedicate to trading, scalping or day trading may not be suitable as they require active monitoring. Consider swing trading or position trading, which allow for more flexibility.

- Risk Tolerance

    If you have a lower risk tolerance, strategies that involve shorter timeframes and smaller profit targets may be more suitable. On the other hand, if you are comfortable with higher risk, strategies that offer potential for larger gains may be appealing.

- ✓ Psychological Traits

    Your psychological makeup plays a significant role in trading success. If you thrive on action and quick decision-making, scalping or breakout trading may suit you. If you prefer a more patient and relaxed approach, swing trading or position trading may be a better fit.

- ✓ Experience Level

    Consider your trading experience when choosing a strategy. Some strategies require a deeper understanding of technical or fundamental analysis, while others may be more suitable for beginners.

Remember, there is no right or wrong strategy. It's about finding the strategy that aligns with your goals, risk tolerance, and personality.

Be willing to adapt and refine your chosen strategy as you gain more experience and market conditions change.

Develop a Trading Plan

Once you have chosen a trading strategy, develop a comprehensive trading plan. A trading plan outlines your approach, risk management rules, entry and exit criteria, and overall trading goals.

It acts as a roadmap that guides your trading decisions and helps you stay disciplined.

Include the following elements in your trading plan:

- ➢ **Strategy Overview:** Describe the chosen strategy and its principles.

- ➢ **Risk Management:** Define your risk management rules, including the maximum risk per trade and overall account risk.

- ➢ **Entry and Exit Criteria**: Specify the criteria for entering and exiting trades, including the use of technical indicators or fundamental analysis.

- ➢ **Timeframes:** Determine the timeframes you will trade and how you will analyze them.

- ➢ **Trade Management:** Define how you will manage trades, including setting profit targets and stop-loss levels.

- ➢ **Journaling and Review:** Include a section for journaling your trades and reviewing their performance. Regularly review your trades to identify strengths, weaknesses, and areas for improvement.

- ➢ **Contingency Plans:** Prepare contingency plans for unexpected market events or changes in strategy performance.

A well-defined trading plan provides structure and helps you stay focused on your strategy and goals.

In conclusion, choosing the right trading strategy is a critical step in forex trading success. By understanding yourself as a trader, exploring different strategies, matching them with your personality and lifestyle, and developing a comprehensive trading plan, you can increase your chances of achieving your trading goals. Remember to stay disciplined, continually learn and adapt, and always evaluate the performance of your chosen strategy to ensure its effectiveness over time.

"Success in forex trading is the result of adapting to changing market conditions and continuously improving your trading strategy."

Ed Seykota

CHAPTER 8

UTILIZING EFFECTIVE ENTRY AND EXIT STRATEGIES

Effective entry and exit strategies are vital components of successful forex trading. They determine the timing of your trades and can significantly impact your profitability.

In this chapter, we explore various entry and exit strategies that you can utilize to enhance your trading performance and maximize your gains.

Entry Strategies

a) **Breakout Entry**

A breakout occurs when the price of a currency pair moves above a significant resistance level or below a significant support level.

Breakout traders aim to enter the market once the breakout is confirmed, expecting a continuation of the price movement in the breakout direction.

They often use technical indicators such as the Average True Range (ATR) or Bollinger Bands to identify potential breakouts.

b) **Pullback Entry**

A pullback entry strategy involves waiting for a temporary reversal or retracement against the prevailing trend. Traders look for areas of support or resistance where the price pulls back before resuming the trend.

This strategy allows traders to enter at a better price and potentially catch the next leg of the trend.

c) **Trendline Break Entry**

Trendlines are drawn by connecting the higher lows in an uptrend or lower highs in a downtrend. Traders wait for a confirmed break of the trendline to enter the market.

This strategy helps traders catch the beginning of a new trend or continuation of an existing one.

d) **Candlestick Patterns**

Candlestick patterns, such as engulfing patterns, harami patterns, or doji patterns, can provide signals for entry. Traders look for specific candlestick formations that indicate a potential reversal or continuation of the price movement.

e) **Indicator-Based Entry**

Many traders rely on technical indicators to generate entry signals.

Popular indicators include moving averages, stochastic oscillators, and Relative Strength Index (RSI). By combining multiple indicators or using them in conjunction with other entry strategies, traders can increase the probability of successful trades.

Exit Strategies

- **Take Profit Orders**

  Take profit orders allow traders to automatically exit a trade when the price reaches a predetermined profit target. It helps lock in gains and eliminates the need for constant monitoring. Traders can set take profit orders based on key support or resistance levels, Fibonacci extensions, or measured move targets.

- **Stop Loss Orders**

  Stop loss orders are used to limit potential losses by automatically exiting a trade if the price moves against the trader's position. Traders determine the appropriate level for the stop loss based on their risk tolerance, technical analysis, or volatility measures such as Average True Range (ATR).

- **Trailing Stop Orders**

  Trailing stops allow traders to protect profits by adjusting the stop loss level as the price moves in their favor.

It follows the price at a fixed distance or based on a certain indicator (e.g., moving average) to lock in profits if the price reverses.

➢ **Time-Based Exits**

Some traders prefer to exit trades based on a predetermined time frame, regardless of the price movement. For example, they may close positions at the end of the trading day or before significant economic announcements to avoid potential volatility.

➢ **Exit Based on Technical Signals**

Traders may choose to exit a trade based on technical signals that indicate a potential reversal or loss of momentum. These signals can include bearish or bullish divergences on oscillators, chart patterns, or trendline breaks in the opposite direction.

➢ **Manual Monitoring**

Experienced traders may prefer to manually monitor their trades and exit based on their analysis of the market conditions. This approach requires active engagement and continuous assessment of the trade's performance.

Combination Strategies

Traders often combine multiple entry and exit strategies to increase their chances of success.

For example, a trader may use a breakout entry strategy to enter a trade and then set a trailing stop order to protect profits and maximize gains if the price continues to move in the desired direction.

It's important to note that no entry or exit strategy guarantees profits in every trade. The key is to find a combination of strategies that align with your trading style, risk tolerance, and market conditions. Regularly evaluate and refine your strategies based on your trading performance and market observations.

Practice and Backtesting

Before implementing any entry or exit strategy in live trading, it's crucial to practice and backtest them. Utilize demo accounts or historical data to test the effectiveness of your strategies. Backtesting allows you to analyze past price data and evaluate the performance of your strategies in different market conditions. It helps you gain confidence in your chosen strategies and make necessary adjustments.

In a nutshell, effective entry and exit strategies are essential for successful forex trading. By combining various entry strategies, setting clear exit rules, and adapting to market conditions, you can enhance your trading performance and increase your profitability.

Remember to practice, backtest, and continually evaluate your strategies to ensure their effectiveness over time.

"The best traders understand that risk management is more important than chasing high returns."

Paul Tudor Jones

CHAPTER 9

MANAGING EMOTIONS AND AVOIDING IMPULSIVE TRADING

Emotions play a significant role in forex trading. The market's dynamic nature, potential for high profits or losses, and the pressure to make quick decisions can evoke a range of emotions in traders. Managing these emotions and avoiding impulsive trading is crucial for maintaining discipline, making rational decisions, and achieving long-term success.

In this chapter, we explore effective strategies to manage emotions and cultivate a mindset that promotes disciplined trading.

Recognize and Understand Emotions

The first step in managing emotions is to recognize and understand them. Common emotions that traders experience include fear, greed, frustration, and excitement. Fear may arise when facing potential losses or uncertainty, while greed can lead to chasing profits or taking excessive risks. Frustration can occur when trades do not go as planned, and excitement may cloud judgment during winning streaks.

By identifying and understanding these emotions, traders can separate them from their decision-making process. It allows for a more objective assessment of market conditions and helps prevent impulsive actions driven by emotions.

Develop a Trading Plan and Stick to It

Having a well-defined trading plan is crucial for managing emotions. A trading plan outlines your strategies, risk management rules, and goals. It acts as a roadmap that guides your trading decisions and helps maintain discipline during volatile market conditions.

Stick to your trading plan, even when emotions run high.

Avoid deviating from the plan due to impulsive reactions. Review and update your trading plan regularly to reflect changes in market dynamics, but always adhere to the core principles and rules you have set for yourself.

Practice Proper Risk Management

Implementing proper risk management techniques is essential for emotional control. Determine the amount of capital you are willing to risk on each trade, and ensure your position sizes align with your risk tolerance.

By limiting the potential loss per trade, you can alleviate the fear of significant financial setbacks. This allows you to focus on the long-term perspective and make rational decisions based on your trading plan, rather than succumbing to impulsive actions driven by fear or greed.

Utilize Stop Loss Orders

Stop loss orders are valuable tools for managing emotions and mitigating losses. By setting a predetermined level at which you will exit a trade if it goes against you, you create a safety net that protects your capital.

Stop loss orders remove the need for constant monitoring and decision-making in rapidly changing market conditions. They provide peace of mind, reducing the emotional stress associated with market fluctuations and allowing you to remain focused on your overall trading strategy.

Practice Patience and Discipline

Patience and discipline are essential virtues for managing emotions in forex trading. Avoid impulsive actions driven by short-term market movements or emotional reactions. Instead, wait for your predefined entry and exit points based on your trading plan.

Exercise patience when waiting for favorable market conditions and be disciplined in executing your trades accordingly. This approach helps minimize emotional influences and promotes a more systematic and objective trading approach.

Utilize Positive Self-Talk and Visualization Techniques

Positive self-talk and visualization techniques can be powerful tools for managing emotions.

Replace negative thoughts or self-doubt with positive affirmations and reinforce your confidence in your trading abilities. Visualize successful trades and positive outcomes. Create mental images of achieving your trading goals and experiencing the feelings of satisfaction and accomplishment. These techniques help reframe your mindset and reinforce a positive attitude towards trading.

Take Breaks and Practice Self-Care

Forex trading can be demanding and mentally exhausting. Taking breaks and practicing self-care are crucial for managing emotions effectively. Engage in activities outside of trading that bring you joy and relaxation.

Exercise regularly, practice mindfulness or meditation, and ensure you get enough restful sleep. Taking care of your physical and mental well-being will help you approach trading with a clear and focused mindset.

Seek Support and Learn from Mistakes

Seeking support from fellow traders or joining trading communities can provide valuable emotional support. Surround yourself with like-minded individuals who understand the challenges of trading and can offer guidance and encouragement.

Additionally, learn from your mistakes and losses. Analyze your trading decisions objectively, identify areas for improvement, and make necessary adjustments.

Viewing losses as opportunities for growth and learning can help you manage emotions and stay motivated.

Summarily, managing emotions and avoiding impulsive trading are essential for long-term success in forex trading. By recognizing and understanding emotions, developing a trading plan, practicing proper risk management, utilizing stop loss orders, practicing patience and discipline, utilizing positive self-talk and visualization techniques, taking breaks and practicing self-care, seeking support, and learning from mistakes, you can cultivate a mindset that promotes disciplined and rational trading decisions. Remember that emotional mastery takes time and practice, but with dedication and self-awareness, you can navigate the forex market with confidence and achieve your trading goals.

"Winning in forex trading requires a balance between risk and reward, knowing when to take profits, and when to cut losses."

George Soros

CHAPTER 10

CONTINUAL LEARNING AND IMPROVEMENT IN FOREX TRADING

Forex trading is a dynamic and ever-evolving field, requiring traders to embrace a mindset of continual learning and improvement. The ability to adapt to changing market conditions, stay updated on new strategies and techniques, and refine your skills is crucial for long-term success.

In this chapter, we explore the importance of continual learning in forex trading and provide valuable tips to help you enhance your trading abilities.

Embrace a Growth Mindset

To foster continual learning and improvement, it's essential to adopt a growth mindset. Embrace the belief that your abilities can be developed through dedication, practice, and a willingness to learn. This mindset allows you to view challenges as opportunities for growth and encourages you to seek new knowledge and skills.

Understand that forex trading is a journey of continuous improvement, and each trading experience provides valuable lessons.

Embrace setbacks as learning experiences and remain committed to enhancing your trading skills.

Stay Updated with Market News and Analysis

Keeping yourself informed about the latest market news, economic events, and geopolitical developments is crucial for effective decision-making in forex trading. Regularly read financial news, follow reputable market analysts, and stay updated on economic calendars.

Understanding the impact of global events on currency movements helps you make informed trading decisions. Utilize reliable sources of information, such as financial news websites, economic research reports, and industry-leading publications, to enhance your market knowledge.

Engage in Ongoing Education

Take advantage of the numerous educational resources available to expand your knowledge of forex trading. Attend webinars, seminars, and workshops conducted by industry experts. Participate in online courses or certification programs that focus on specific aspects of trading, such as technical analysis, fundamental analysis, or risk management.

Read books written by successful traders and industry professionals to gain insights into their strategies and experiences. Join trading communities or forums where you can engage in discussions and share knowledge with fellow traders.

Analyze and Review Your Trades

Regularly analyze and review your trading performance to identify strengths, weaknesses, and areas for improvement. Keep a trading journal where you record your trades, including entry and exit points, reasons for entering the trade, and any emotional or psychological factors that influenced your decision-making.

Review your trades objectively, looking for patterns, trends, and areas where you can make adjustments. Identify successful strategies and replicate them while learning from mistakes to avoid repeating them in the future. Continuous analysis and review of your trades help you refine your trading approach and increase your chances of success.

Utilize Simulated Trading or Demo Accounts

Simulated trading or demo accounts provide a risk-free environment for practicing and testing new strategies. These accounts use virtual funds to replicate real-time market conditions, allowing you to hone your skills and gain confidence without risking actual capital.

Utilize demo accounts to implement new techniques, test different trading strategies, and familiarize yourself with various trading platforms. Monitor your performance, evaluate the effectiveness of different strategies, and make adjustments as necessary before transitioning to live trading.

Network with Experienced Traders

Networking with experienced traders can provide valuable insights and perspectives.

Attend trading conferences, join professional trading organizations, and participate in online forums or social media groups dedicated to forex trading.

Engage in meaningful conversations, ask questions, and learn from the experiences of others.

Connecting with experienced traders allows you to tap into their knowledge, gain new perspectives, and discover advanced trading techniques.

Emphasize Risk Management

Continual learning in forex trading also involves strengthening your risk management skills.

Understand and implement effective risk management techniques, such as setting appropriate stop-loss orders, determining position sizes based on risk-reward ratios, and diversifying your trading portfolio.

Regularly assess your risk tolerance and adjust your risk management strategies accordingly.

Learn about advanced risk management techniques, such as trailing stops, hedging, and portfolio optimization, to protect your capital and minimize losses.

Maintain a Healthy Work-Life Balance

Maintaining a healthy work-life balance is essential for continual learning and improvement in forex trading.

Avoid overtrading or becoming excessively consumed by the markets. Allow yourself time to rest, rejuvenate, and pursue interests outside of trading.

A well-rested and balanced mind is more receptive to learning and can make better trading decisions. Take breaks, engage in hobbies, spend time with loved ones, and prioritize self-care to ensure your overall well-being and long-term success in trading.

In a nutshell, continual learning and improvement are integral to success in forex trading. By embracing a growth mindset, staying updated with market news, engaging in ongoing education, analyzing and reviewing your trades, utilizing simulated trading accounts, networking with experienced traders, emphasizing risk management, and maintaining a healthy work-life balance, you can enhance your trading abilities and adapt to changing market conditions.

Remember, forex trading is a lifelong journey of growth and improvement, and the commitment to learning is the key to unlocking your full potential as a trader.

THE END